Circle of Prayer

For Flora.
You inspired us.

Compilation copyright © 2003 Joyce Denham
All unattributed prayers copyright ©
Joyce Denham
This edition copyright © 2003 Lion Publishing

The moral rights of the author
have been asserted

Published by
Lion Publishing plc
Mayfield House, 256 Banbury Road,
Oxford OX2 7DH, England
www.lion-publishing.co.uk
ISBN 0 7459 4782 4

First edition 2003
10 9 8 7 6 5 4 3 2 1

Typeset in 12/14 Lapidary 333 BT
Printed and bound in Spain
by Bookprint S.L.

Carmina Gadelica collected by Alexander
Carmichael is published by Floris Books,
Edinburgh.

Acknowledgments
Scripture quotations pp. 9, 32 (except
Psalm 128:1), 34, 41 and 61 taken from
the Holy Bible, New International Version,
copyright © 1973, 1978, 1984 by
International Bible Society. Used by
permission of Hodder & Stoughton Limited.
All rights reserved. 'NIV' is a registered
trademark of International Bible Society.
UK trademark number 1448790.

Scripture quotations pp. 32 (Psalm 128:1)
and 77 are taken from the Holy Bible,
New Living Translation, copyright © 1996.
Used by permission of Tyndale House
Publishers, Inc., Wheaton, Illinois 60189.
All rights reserved.

Extract p. 37 from the Authorized Version
of the Bible (The King James Bible), the
rights in which are vested in the Crown, is
reproduced by permission of the Crown's
Patentee, Cambridge University Press.

The Scripture quotation on p. 33 is from
The New Revised Standard Version of the
Bible, Anglicized Edition, copyright © 1989,
1995 by the Division of Christian Education
of the National Council of the Churches of
Christ in the United States of America, and
is used by permission. All rights reserved.

Circle of Prayer

Prayers and blessings
in the Celtic tradition

Written and compiled by
Joyce Denham

A LION BOOK

Contents

Special Blessings and Concerns

Author's Note

Hundreds of years ago, Celtic Christians in Ireland and Scotland began their mornings with prayer. They woke up asking God to bless the new day. They prayed as they brought the fire back to life, and as they splashed water on their faces, dressed and ate their breakfasts. Throughout the entire day they prayed – as they walked, swept, gardened, wove cloth, cooked, ate, and tended the animals. Their prayers were full of references to nature and to the Trinity – God revealed in three different ways, as God the Father, God the Son (who is Jesus) and God the Holy Spirit. Terms of affection for the Trinity, such as My Great Three and My Three of Love, were common. Sometimes these medieval Christians recited their prayers aloud together; sometimes they muttered them quietly so no one but God could hear; and often they sang or chanted them to lively, rhythmic tunes. In any case, from morning till evening they sensed God's presence, through every week and season of the year.

For centuries these prayers were passed from one generation to the next through oral tradition. Even though they were not written down, simple rhymes and metres made them easy to memorize. A person might know hundreds of them, having prayer-poems for every day and occasion; they formed a commonly held treasure of personal and corporate devotion, although they varied slightly from family to family and village to village.

Eventually, political instability, together with famine and disease, led to widespread emigration and suppression of the

Gaelic language. The rich legacy of oral prayers fell more and more into disuse so that by the nineteenth century the prayers were in danger of extinction. Hundreds of them were rescued and preserved by a Scot named Alexander Carmichael, who devoted many years of his life to writing them down and translating them into English. He published them in a set of several volumes called *Carmina Gadelica* – Gaelic songs or hymns. Translation is always a difficult task, but translation of poetry even more so. The translator must choose either to preserve a sense of rhythm and rhyme, thus losing accuracy of meaning, or strive for accuracy of meaning, thus losing rhythm and rhyme. Carmichael chose the latter. His translations are brilliant in showing us what exactly these ancient prayers say, but they lack the delightful rhymes and metres that were such an integral part of their use. Nevertheless, their open-hearted spirit, their references to God's presence in creation and their invitation to true intimacy and friendship with God are profound and compelling. They are now part of a widespread movement to introduce Christians to a more personal, simple and grace-infused prayer life – one in which God becomes present in the smallest activities of life.

This book contains selections, some with modernized language, from *Carmina Gadelica,* and new prayers that I have written in the tradition of the old. I hope that the simple rhymes and metres I adopted will not only suggest the flavour of the originals, but will make these new prayers easy to repeat and memorize. I hope too that you will find yourself repeating them as you go about your daily tasks – perhaps even passing them on to others through your own oral tradition. That is, after all, how they were meant to be used.

Most of all, I hope that all of these prayers will lead you into deeper intimacy with God, and that you will sense God walking with you in every step and through every day.

Joyce Denham

Daily Prayers

The day is yours, and yours also the night;

you established the sun and moon.

Psalm 74:16

Morning Prayers

New Light

O God, who brought me from the rest of last night
To the joyous light of this day,
Bring me from the new light of this day
To the guiding light of eternity.

Carmina Gadelica

Rising Prayer

King of moon, great king of sun,
King of starlight, Three in One,

Waken me in newborn dawn,
Night is fading, tired and drawn.

See me needy, poor, undressed,
Wrap me in your garments blessed.

Clothe me, tailor from above,
Weaver of the garb of love.

Rip the tattered hate and scorn,
Selfish habits overworn.

Loom new fabrics, true and fine,
Interweave your heart with mine.

So in rising I shall be
Clothed in royal finery.

God to Cover Me

I cover myself today
With God's almighty love.

I clothe myself with grace
And patience from above.

With Triune power of truth,
My willing feet are shod.

Heaven's wisdom crowns my head
And leads my soul to God.

Lighting the Fire

In ancient times, the woman of the home recited this prayer
as she brought the fire back to life in the morning. It's still a
wonderful prayer to use when lighting a candle, switching on
the fire, or boiling the kettle.

I will kindle my fire this morning
In the presence of the holy angels of heaven.

God kindle in my heart within
A flame of love to my neighbour,
To my foe, to my friend, to my kindred all,
From the lowliest thing that lives,
To the Name that is highest of all.

Carmina Gadelica

A Bathing Prayer

Bathing prayers were common. Even the most mundane
task became an opportunity to commit oneself to God.
A prayer like this one would be recited as each palmful
of water was splashed over the body. Bathing prayers also
served as reminders of baptism.

For will and thoughts unwed,
A palmful on my head.

For radiance of grace,
A palmful on my face.

For tasks that life demands,
A palmful on my hands.

For strength against alarms,
A palmful on my arms.

For fight and for retreat,
A palmful on my feet.

For love in every part,
A palmful on my heart.

Disciples' feet you bathe;
Wash all of me instead;*

My heart, my being lave,
My feet, my hands, my head.

* One night before their dinner, Jesus washed his disciples'
feet. But Peter refused, not wanting Jesus to be his servant.
Jesus explained, 'If I don't wash your feet, you can have no
part with me.' Peter replied, 'Then don't stop with my feet,
but wash my hands and my head as well!'

Morning Praise

Loving Creator,
You awaken me
To new life
Every morning;
Your faithfulness
Is so great,
It is deeper than the sea,
Higher than the sky,
Wider than the world.

Be near me,
Within me,
Beside me,
This day
And for ever.
Amen.

I Believe

I believe, O Lord and God of the peoples,
That you are the creator of the high heavens,
That you are the creator of the skies above,
That you are the creator of the oceans below.

Carmina Gadelica

Bless Me Today

Bless to me, O God, my work this day.
For love in all my labours, first I pray.

Bless all my speech, my mind and thoughts renew;
Let my beliefs be joined to what I do.

Then bless to me, O God, my heart's desire:
That humble tasks burn with creative fire.

Bless all that I encounter on my way,
And all I see and hear; bless me today.

Seeing, Hearing, Saying

Bless,
O God,
What I see
With my eyes,
And bless
What I see
In my mind.

Bless,
O God,
What I hear
With my ears,
And bless
What I hear
In my heart.

Bless,
O God,
What I say
With my lips,
And bless
What I say
In my deeds.

God Bless the World

God, bless the world and all that is therein.
God, bless my spouse and my children,
God, bless the eye that is in my head,
And bless, O God, the handling of my hand;
From the time I rise in the morning early,
To the time I lie down late in bed;
Bless my rising in the morning early,
And my lying down late in bed.

Carmina Gadelica

Morning Meditation

Sun rises
Light surprises
Mist dispels
Lark tells

Day follows night
Promise follows plight
Life follows death
Breath follows breath

World twists
God exists
Earth spins
God wins

Evening Prayers

Evening prayers are said at bedtime, asking for God's blessing all through the night.

At Sunset

Now falls the sun
Far out of sight;
Now comes the night
With little light;

Yet well I know
Sun's certain rise,
Climbing upon
Grey morning skies;

So, gracious God,
Your grace will be
Ever reborn
In such as me.

Evening Prayer

Orion
And the Pleiades
Were set aloft by you;

The brightness
Of the brightest day
You change to moonlit hue;

The failing
Lamp of morn you quench
At sound of evening's call;

Let all with breath
Seek you, most blest,
Great God, O Lord of All.

Based on Amos 5:8

Night Shield

God shield the house, the stores, the kin,
And everyone who dwells herein.

God shield me and my loved ones all,
Build round our lives your solid wall

Of truth and goodness, love and light,
Preserving us from evil's blight.

Deliver us, O God of might,
Through every day and every night.

The Lord's My Shepherd

The Lord's my shepherd,
I'm his sheep.
We rest near waters
Quiet and deep.

He leads me
On the narrow track,
And when I stumble,
Pulls me back.

He's in the valley
At my side,
When death is near
And I can't hide.

His rod and staff
Protecting me,
I will not fear,
Nor will I flee.

Behind the rocks
Are hungry spies;
He spreads a feast
Before their eyes.

Healing ointments
Crown my head;
I, rich with blessings,
Go to bed.

Loving kindness
Leaves me never,
I am in his fold
For ever.

Based on Psalm 23

Night Prayer

The sacred Three
To save,
To shield,
To surround
The hearth,
The house,
The household,
This eve,
This night,
Oh! this eve,
This night,
And every night,
Each single night.
Amen.

Carmina Gadelica

Locking the Door

As I lock my door this night,
May I lock the door to evil
   In my home,
   In my heart,
   In my speech,
   In my deeds.

As I lock my door this night,
May I lock God's love inside
   In my home,
   In my heart,
   In my speech,
   In my deeds.

Guardian Angel

Bright angel
Who has care of me,
Guard all my sleep
And reverie,

While from God's face
You turn your gaze
To watch o'er mine
Through all my days.

Enfold me,
Servant from above,
Agent of God's
Far-reaching love.

On seas of trouble,
Save my boat
From reef and shoal.
Keep it afloat.

Be guiding star,
And hold the oar,
And shelter me
Till safe ashore,

This day,
This night,
In every swell,
Until in heaven's port I dwell.

Christ with Me Sleeping

Christ with me sleeping,
Christ with me waking,
Christ with me watching,
Each day and night.

God with me protecting,
The Lord with me directing,
The Spirit with me strengthening,
For ever and for evermore.

Carmina Gadelica

I Lie Down this Night

I lie down this night with God,
And God will lie down with me;
I lie down this night with Christ,
And Christ will lie down with me;
I lie down this night with the Spirit,
And the Spirit will lie down with me;
God and Christ and the Spirit
Be lying down with me.

Carmina Gadelica

Going to Bed

May the Light of lights come
To my dark heart from your place;
May the Spirit's wisdom come
To my heart's tablet from my Saviour.

Be the peace of the Spirit mine this night,
Be the peace of the Son mine this night,
Be the peace of the Father mine this night,
The peace of all peace be mine this night,
Each morning and evening of my life.

Carmina Gadelica

The Gifts of the Three

Spirit, give me of your abundance,
Father, give me of your wisdom,
Son, give me in my need,
Jesus beneath the shelter of your shield.

I lie down tonight,
With the Triune of my strength,
With the Father, with Jesus,
With the Spirit of might.

Carmina Gadelica

Bless Me This Night

Father, bless me in my body,
Father, bless me in my soul;
Father, bless me this night
In my body and in my soul.

Carmina Gadelica

Turning Out the Light

Out goes the sun,
Out goes the day,
Out goes my lamp –
The night's delay.

Now light of heaven,
Now lamp of soul,
Now God above
Shines bright below.

Table Graces

Blessing Before Meals

O Christ,
When you blessed the crowd,
Tired and hungry,

Five loaves and two fishes
Became banquet dishes.

O Christ,
At the poor father's
Grand wedding party,

Great vats of plain water
Gave wine for his daughter.

Now Christ,
As you bless us all,
Grant us our wishes:

Change hearts small and empty
To signs of your plenty.

At Meals

We give great thanks
For food,
For drink,
For breath of air,
For Three sustaining everywhere.

In what we eat,
In what we drink,
In what we say,
In what we think,
May thanks and praise
For ever be
To gracious, loving Trinity.
Amen.

Table Grace I

Food-giver,
Drink-giver,
Life-giver,
Love-giver,
Spirit-giver,

We thank you for
Your bountiful,
Never-ceasing gifts
To us your creatures.
Amen.

Table Grace II

Thanks be to God our Father
For bread to nourish our bodies,
And for Jesus, the Bread of Life.

Thanks be to God our Father
For water to sustain our bodies,
And for Jesus, the Water of Life.

May our true food and drink
Be to do your will,
As Jesus did on earth,
As Jesus does in heaven.
Amen.

Thanks After Food

Thanks be to you, O God,
Praise be to you, O God,
Reverence be to you, O God,
For all you have given me.

Carmina Gadelica

Blessing on Work

Bless, O loving God,
My work this day.
May I work as your partner,
Caring for the world,
Creating anew;
For at the dawn of life
Your Spirit hovered
Over the waters and laboured
To bring forth trees and mountains
And every living thing.
May I work as Adam worked,
Naming each creature,
Calling it to become what you planned.
Give me patience
To bear what is unpleasant;
Strength to meet demands;
Forgiveness towards those
Who wrong me;
Integrity in my dealings;
Tenderness towards all
Your creatures,
That in some small way
I and others may taste of Eden
Until I dwell in your new heavens
And your new earth,
And all my work is fulfilled.

In the name of the Three of Life.
Amen.

Blessing on Rest

Bless, O Sabbath God,
My rest today.
May it be done to tend
And repair your creation –
For after six days of work,
You rested,
Blessing the Sabbath
And making it holy.
O Sabbath God,
Let me not fail to rest,
For if I do, I have failed
To complete my work.

May I rest with joy
In your creation,
In your goodness,
In your presence.

May it be a sweet taste
Of that promised rest with you,
At the end of earth's labours,
The dawn of paradise.
Amen.

Walking Prayers

Walking prayers are part of an ancient tradition of Christian pilgrimage. Repeat these short, simple prayers as you walk, letting the words fall into the rhythm of your steps. As you walk, God walks beside you.

God, bless the path on which I go,
God, bless the earth beneath my sole.

Carmina Gadelica

Father above me,
Son beside me,
Spirit within me,
The Three all around me.

Who is before me?
Who is behind me?
Who is beneath me?
God and the Lord.

Carmina Gadelica

Breathe on me,
Breath of day and night;
Shine in my heart,
My Three of Light.

My walk this day with God,
My walk this day with Christ,
My walk this day with Spirit,
The Threefold all-kindly:
Ho! ho! ho! the Threefold all-kindly.

Carmina Gadelica

Show me your ways, O Lord,
  teach me your paths.

Psalm 25:4

Your word is a lamp to my feet
  and a light for my path.

Psalm 119:105

Though I walk in the midst of trouble,
  you preserve my life.

Psalm 138:7

Let us walk in the light of the Lord.

Isaiah 2:5

How happy are those who fear the Lord –
  all who follow his ways!

Psalm 128:1

Psalms

The Psalms of the Bible are ancient Hebrew prayer-poems. They formed the main prayer book of the Christian Church during the Middle Ages. The psalms that follow are expressions of praise to the wondrous and ever-loving God of creation.

God's Majesty

O Lord, our Sovereign,
  how majestic is your name in all the earth!

You have set your glory above the heavens.
  Out of the mouths of babes and infants
you have founded a bulwark because of your foes,
  to silence the enemy and the avenger.

When I look at your heavens, the work of your fingers,
  the moon and the stars that you have established;
what are human beings that you are mindful of them,
  mortals that you care for them?

Yet you have made them a little lower than God,
  and crowned them with glory and honour.

You have given them dominion over the works of your hands;
  you have put all things under their feet,
all sheep and oxen,
  and also the beasts of the field,

the birds of the air, and the fish of the sea,
    whatever passes along the paths of the seas.

O Lord, our Sovereign,
    how majestic is your name in all the earth!

Psalm 8

O God, You Light Up My Darkness

I love you, O Lord, my strength.

The Lord is my rock, my fortress and my deliverer;
    my God is my rock, in whom I take refuge.
    He is my shield and the horn of my salvation,
        my stronghold.
I will call to the Lord, who is worthy of praise,
    and I am saved from my enemies.

You, O Lord, keep my lamp burning;
    my God turns my darkness into light.

Psalm 18:1–3, 28

The Glory of Creation

'Glory to God!' the heavens declare.
'What God has made is everywhere!'
Day after day they speak the word,
Night after night their voice is heard.
All round the world it's understood
The heavens are shouting, 'God is good!'
For in them God has made a dome
Through which the blazing sun may roam.
The earth cannot escape his heat,
Robed in God's glory all complete.
'See God's great love!' the heavens declare.
'God's light is shining everywhere!'

Based on Psalm 19:1–6

God's Wonders

Listener to prayers,
Love of the poor,
To earth's vast ends,
Far ocean's shore;

Across the world
Your wonders shine,
From break of dawn
To sun's decline:

You raise your arm,
The mountains soar;
You speak and hush
The wild sea's roar;

You thunder,
Nations leave their pride,
Neighbour with neighbour
To abide.

Wherever day
To earth belongs,
Let all with voice
Sing joyous songs!

Based on Psalm 65

God Reigns

Rightly God reigns o'er all the earth,
Strength is God's shield and God's rod;
   Majesty is God's glorious robe,
   For ever and ever is God.

Still the seas shout with crashing waves,
Lifting their voices on high;
   Mightier than their thundering roar,
   God tames the sea and the sky.

How you endure! How firm your laws!
Your goodness in heaven is stored.
   Eternity is your endless house,
   For ever and ever, O Lord.

Based on Psalm 93

King Above All Gods

O come, let us sing unto the Lord:
let us make a joyful noise to the rock of our salvation.

For the Lord is a great God,
and a great King above all gods.

In his hand are the deep places of the earth:
the strength of the hills is his also.

The sea is his, and he made it:
and his hands formed the dry land.

O come, let us worship and bow down:
let us kneel before the Lord our maker.

Psalm 95:1, 3–6

Shout to the Lord!

Shout, O earth, to the Lord!
Lift up your hands and applaud!
With gladness, worship and awe,
Raising your praises to God.

For God is Lord over all,
Who made us, to whom we belong;
In God's pastures we are God's sheep,
God's people, God's work and God's song.

Approach heaven's gates with deep thanks
And fill heaven's courts with rich praise
For God's holy being and breath,
God's name and mysterious ways.

For God is good and is love,
Is faithful and never forsakes,
In all generations assures,
Redeems, renews and remakes.

Based on Psalm 100

Simple Praise

Praise the Lord now, all you nations,
Peoples, persons and relations.
Praise the Lord with glad oration:
Love for all! Such exultation!

Based on Psalm 117

All Creation Sings

Hallelujah!
Praise God, every being on high.
Praise! You angels of the sky.

Praise God, sun and moon and star,
Shining on us from afar.

Praise! You waters overhead,
Hovering o'er your earthly bed.

Shout for joy, all things above,
Made by God's eternal love,

Set in place by God's decree,
Always, ever you shall be.

Praise God from the earth below,
Lightning, hail, rain and snow,

Winds that howl at God's behest,
Fishes, seas and ocean depths,

Fells and mountains, trees and plains,
Creatures wild and creatures tame.

From beetle bugs in armour-plates,
To kings and queens and potentates,

From young to old and in-between,
Praise the God of breath and being,

Whose splendour soars above the sky,
Calling to earth in grand reply.

Praise to God's name exalted high.
Hallelujah! Hallelujah!

Hallelujah cry!

Based on Psalm 148

Festivals and Seasons

It was you who set all the

boundaries of the earth;

you made both summer and winter.

Psalm 74:17

The Four Seasons

Spring

Now creation's Chief
Calls bud and leaf,
While all in number
Rise from slumber.

Dry, cold earth awakes,
God's quickening takes;
So begins the trade:
Bent stem for blade;

Withered rose for flow'r;
Spring drought for show'r;
And oh, the fragrance sweet
Of life complete.

Just so, tender Chief,
Raise my belief.
See how it sprouts new green;
Fat stalks from lean.

Summer

Now Sun's arms
Stretch long, unfold;
More of God-light to behold.

Short the night,
Twice long the day;
Father, Son and Spirit, stay.

Languid hours,
Sweet, peaceful rest;
All of nature is God's guest.

Warm as earth,
Souls take God's ease;
Fall in worship on our knees.

Autumn

Now the fruits of
Life and labour
Drop like gold,
Are ours to savour.

Palette pigments,
Red and crimson,
Burst from hiding,
Find their season.

Gasp of life,
Earth in her glory,
All to end the
Year's long story.

O Autumn,
How you play this part
To sate my soul,
Yet break my heart.

Still, in your beauty
I can see,
God's promise of
Eternity.

Winter

Now marches Winter,
Cruel and stark;
Bitter the winds,
The cold, the dark.

There waltzes Moonbeam,
Shimmering bright,
Promise of God
In Winter's night.

Come, Lord of triumph,
Sunburst and flame,
Darkness defeat,
Wild Winter tame.

Advent

Advent means the arrival of something wonderful. During this season — the four Sundays before Christmas — Christians wait for the birth of Jesus in Bethlehem, the appearance of God on earth. As they wait, they pray for God's light to arrive in their own lives.

Advent Prayer

O come, thou Wisdom, from on high,
And order all things far and nigh:
To us the path of knowledge show,
And teach us in her ways to go.

O come, thou Day-spring, come and cheer
Our spirits by thine advent here;
Disperse the gloomy clouds of night,
And death's dark shadows put to flight.

O come, Desire of nations, bind
In one the hearts of all mankind;
Bid every strife and sorrow cease
And fill the world with heaven's peace.

Veni, veni, Emmanuel *13th century, based on the Advent 'O' Antiphons,
translated by John Mason Neale (1818–66) and others*

Waiting for God

Dark though the night,
The watchmen wait
For hint of light,
For morning's cue.

Dark though my soul,
I also wait.
To make me whole,
I wait for you.

For you, O God,
I long and pray,
And wait
As watchmen wait for day.
No, more than they!
More than the watchmen
Wait for day,
I wait for you,
O God, my stay.

Based on Psalm 130

Christmas

The season of Advent ends with the birth of Jesus – the light of the world has arrived. Christmas is the church's feast in celebration of the birth of Jesus, the Christ.

Christmas Eve

Come, thou Redeemer of the earth,
And manifest thy virgin-birth:
Let every age adoring fall,
Such birth befits the God of all.

Thy cradle here shall glitter bright,
And darkness glow with new-born light,
No more shall night extinguish day,
Where love's bright beams their power display.

St Ambrose (340–97), translated by John Mason Neale and others

Born Tonight!

Born tonight!
In babe the God-heart beats;
Young Mary, all amazed,
Sweet silence keeps.

Born tonight!
All nature stirs with joy;
Creator-God appears
In tiny boy.

Born tonight!
God with us! Can it be
A stable is the door
To worlds heavenly?

Nativity

Tender Trinity,
Threefold love of old,
Triune ancient might,
By prophets told –

O Mighty Three,
Enclosed for me
Within such small
Humanity –

Star bursts in wonder,
Angel sings,
When Godhead moves
With earthly things.

Christmas Chant

This ancient chant was sung by villagers parading
through the streets early on Christmas morning.

Hail King! hail King!
Blessed is He! blessed is He!
Ho, hail! blessed the King!
Ho, hi! let there be joy!

Carmina Gadelica

Mary's Son

Walk with me, fair Mary's Son,
Make my way a blessed one.

Feast with me, kind Mary's Boy,
Fill my soul with heavenly joy.

Speak with me, sweet Mary's Child,
Teach me holy words and mild.

Rest with me, dear Mary's Lad,
Calm my spirit, make me glad.

For if with Mary's Son I be,
My soul dwells with the Trinity.

New Year

As one year ends and another begins, we take time to
review our lives. It is a time to thank God, the creator
of all our days and years, for the gift of each day, for new
days to come, and for the promise of eternal life with
the God who loves us.

New Year's Prayer

Great Maker of the year,
Old Time by you begun,
Each day, each minute and each hour,
All passing one by one,

Through all my time be near.
Oh, guide me with your hand.
My hours are steps, my days are roads
To your sweet timeless land.

St Patrick's Day
17 March

St Patrick was a Roman Briton born in the year 389. When
he was sixteen years old, Irish sea pirates kidnapped him
and sold him in Ireland as a slave. Eventually he escaped,
but years later he returned to Ireland and spent the rest of
his life there spreading the message of Christ's love.

In strength of sky and depth of sea,
I place my faith in God the Three.
With threefold might protecting me
I rise in strength of Trinity.
Christ on my right
Christ on my left
Christ in the heights
Christ in the depths.
Behind, before,
Within, without,
Christ's power to compass me about.
Christ's ear to hear
Christ's eye to see
Christ's mind in all who think of me.

Adapted from 'The Deer's Cry', a prayer attributed to St Patrick

Lent

Lent comes from an old word meaning spring. In the
Christian Church, it's the forty days before Easter.
During Lent, Christians renew their own commitment
to God and give thanks for God's love and forgiveness.

Lenten Prayer

Throughout the forty days of Lent, begin and end
each day with this prayer. Follow the prayer with a
period of silence, simply sitting in God's presence.

As your own angels,
As your own saints,
As your own household
Desire in heaven,
So may I desire on earth!

Carmina Gadelica

Easter

Easter is the name of the feast celebrating Jesus'
resurrection. Three days after Jesus was crucified by
Roman rulers, he rose from the dead – offering new
life to the whole world.

Christ the Conqueror

Thanks be to you, victorious Christ,
Breaking the bars to heaven's room,
Defeating evil, death and gloom:
For ever in your empty tomb
Lock them, O conqueror of doom.
Ignite, O rising Son, hope's blaze,
Ending earth's nights in glorious days.

Trinity Sunday
Eighth Sunday after Easter

Christians believe that God is three in one – God the
Father, God the Son (who is Jesus the Christ) and God the
Holy Spirit – one God coming to us in three different ways.
Trinity Sunday is a special day to give thanks for the God
who is Three in One.

Holy Trinity

The Three Who are over me,
The Three Who are below me,
The Three Who are above me here,
The Three Who are above me yonder;
The Three Who are in the earth,
The Three Who are in the air,
The Three Who are in the heaven,
The Three Who are in the great pouring sea.

Carmina Gadelica

The Three

In name of Father,
In name of Son,
In name of Spirit,
Three in One:

Father cherish me,
Son cherish me,
Spirit cherish me,
Three all-kindly.

Carmina Gadelica

The Great Three

Three above me overhead,
Three upon the path I tread,
Three who fill the boundless earth,
Three in crashing wave and firth,
Three who are enfolding me,
Three, for all eternity.

St Columba's Day
9 June

Columba was an Irish priest who lived from 521 to 597. When
he was forty years old, he dropped his small boat into the Irish
Sea and prayed that God would take him to the place of God's
choosing. He landed on the tiny island of Iona, off the west coast
of Scotland. From there Columba spread the message of Christ's
love all over Scotland, England and beyond.

Song for Columba

I cast my small boat upon the sea,
To know where God will carry me;
Oarless, I cannot choose my way;
God is my oar both night and day.

The shore recedes, the waves grow high;
I'm tossed between the sea and sky;
Companionless in my retreat,
God is the one I've come to meet.

No earthen walls, no friends, no kin;
No little hut to seal me in;
My ocean is a desert wide;
I'm shelterless and cannot hide.

I seek God in the ancient tides;
I heed the heavens where God resides;
Within the mist, in Trinity,
I sense God's presence heeding me.

God moves within the darkening sky;
God stirs the depths on which I lie;
God comes to me upon the sea;
God's all around, and breathes on me;

Whose hand is underneath my boat;
Who bears it up, keeps it afloat;
Who marks the place where it will land
And sets me safe where it was planned.

Here on this tiny windswept isle
I make a home in Godly style;
And every day that I am given,
I greet the God of earth and heaven.

I chant in rhythm to the sea;
I sing unto the Mighty Three;
In wind and wave I hear God's voice;
One foot in heaven, I now rejoice.

Here other pilgrims seeking rest
Can pray and worship and be blest;
And with God's Spirit here I'll stay,
Until my Resurrection Day.

Harvest Thanksgiving

Great God,
God of harvest,
Heads of grain are full,
Fruit drops rich from trees,
Fields wave gold and green;

    The Cosmic Gardener moves unseen.

Great God,
God of creation,
Yours are the grains,
Yours are the trees,
Yours are the fields;

    The Cosmic Gardener gives the yields.

Great God,
Rich as Eden's home,
Harvest time is come;
Abundant food, drink,
Rest; the fat of land;

    The Cosmic Gardener's open hand.

All Saints' Day
1 November

On this day, Christians remember all the faithful who let the light of Christ's love shine in their lives.

For Saints Everywhere

When I shall arrive at heaven's wide gates,
I'll praise you, O God, with all of your saints:

Mary and Martha, Christ's dear family friends;
Paul, who persuaded with parchment and pens;

Peter and Andrew, such brave fisherfolk;
Martin, who gave an old beggar his cloak;

Francis, the rich man who wanted God more;
Bridget, who cared for the sick and the poor.

When I shall arrive at heaven's wide gates,
I'll praise you, O God, with all of your saints,

The rich ones, the poor ones, the strong and the spent,
Who held forth the Christ-light wherever they went.

Special Blessings and Concerns

Keep me safe, O God,

for in you I take refuge.

Psalm 16:1

Baptism

Baptism Prayer for a Child

The parent can recite this prayer to their child before the baptism, and on the anniversaries of the child's baptism.

O Being who inhabits the heights,
Impart your blessing early,
Remember the child of my body,
In name of the Father of peace;

When the priest of the King of heaven
Puts on (name) the water of meaning,
Grant (him/her)
The blessing of the Three
Who fill the heights.
The blessing of the Three
Who fill the heights.

Sprinkle down on (name) your grace,
Give to (him/her) virtue and growth,
Give to (him/her) strength and guidance,
Sense and reason,
Angel wisdom in (his/her) day,
That (he/she) may stand without reproach
In your presence.
That (he/she) may stand without reproach
In your presence.

Carmina Gadelica

Birth Baptism

This prayer is part of an old tradition performed at the birth of a child. The midwife placed three drops of water on the forehead of the newborn infant, saying these words:

In name of Father,
Amen.
In name of Son,
Amen.
In name of Spirit,
Amen.

Three to lave thee,
Amen.
Three to bathe thee,
Amen.
Three to save thee,
Amen.

Father and Son and Spirit,
Amen.
Father and Son and Spirit,
Amen.
Father and Son and Spirit,
Amen.

Carmina Gadelica

Adult Baptism

God, my healer,
God, my redeemer,
As I place myself beneath the
Waters of baptism,
May I die to sin,
May I die to everything
Within and without
That keeps me from you.

May I rise to new life,
To Christ's life;
May I walk with you
In the light of truth
This day,
All my days,
Until I dwell with you in heaven.

In the name of Father, Son and Spirit,
All holy.
Amen.

Birthdays

Birthday Prayer

Parents, family and friends can use this prayer together at a birthday celebration. Simply insert the person's name where indicated.

Thank you, God, for (_____ 's/my own) birth;
Thank you, God, for making (him/her/me);
Thank you for (his/her/my) boundless worth
From your creativity.

In your mind (he/she/I) had (his/her/my) start;
How you wanted (him/her/me) to be!
(He's/she's/I'm) your special piece of art;
Oh, such possibility.

Confession and Forgiveness

Sit quietly in God's presence for a few minutes. Then begin confession with this prayer adapted from Psalm 19:12–14.

Forgive Me, Lord

O Lord,
My secret and my open faults
Forgive, and grant me blameless thoughts.
Of all my heart and mind take stock,
Oh, let me please you, God, my rock.

Especially forgive me for (*here name particular confessions*).

Sit quietly in God's presence for a few more minutes. Close by repeating the same prayer:

O Lord,
My secret and my open faults
Forgive, and grant me blameless thoughts.
Of all my heart and mind take stock,
Oh, let me please you, God, my rock.
Amen.

Death

Death of a Friend or Loved One

O Christ,

On its way
This soul shall rest,
Cradled by
The saints now blest.

Michael,
Angel-king on high,
Clears the path
To travel by.

Then in heaven
Such welcome sweet,
From the shepherd
Of the sheep.

O God, Be with Me

Grant me grace throughout my life,
Grant me life at the hour of my death;
Be with me, O God, in casting off my breath,
O God, be with me in the deep currents.

O! in the parting of the breath,
O! be with my soul in the deep currents.
O God, be with my soul in sounding the fords,
In crossing the deep floods.

Carmina Gadelica

When Death is Near

I lie in my bed
So near the grave;
God's arms will cradle,
God's arms will save.

Angels are watching,
Breathing with me;
Ready with God's breath,
Tenderly.

Beloved physician
Christ's salve applies
To heart, mind and soul,
To ears and eyes.

Victor physician,
Your balm is fine;
Earth's healing completed,
Heaven's health is mine.

Devotion

God My Hope

I place in you my hope, O God,
My living hope in the Father of the heavens,
My great hope to be with you
In the distant world to come.

Father and Son and Spirit,
The One Person in Three,
Perfect, world without end,
Changeless through life eternal.

Carmina Gadelica

Giving to God

I am giving you love with my whole devotion,
I am giving you kneeling with my whole desire,
I am giving you love with my whole heart,
I am giving you affection with my whole sense;
I am giving you my existence with my whole mind,
I am giving you my soul, O God of all gods.

Carmina Gadelica

Jesu, Creator

Jesu,
Spark of existence,
Poet of the cosmos,
Author of creation's book,
Energizer of the elements,
Force within atoms,
Shaper of molecules,
Breath of life,
Founder of the ages,
Knowledge of the mysteries,
Wisdom herself,
Image of the invisible God,
Lover of mortals,
Forgiver of sins,
Victor over evil,
Conqueror of death,
Saviour of humans,
Friend of humans,
My friend,
My very own friend.
Amen.

God to Enfold Me

God to enfold me,
God to surround me,
God in my speaking,
God in my thinking.

God in my sleeping,
God in my waking,
God in my watching,
God in my hoping.

God in my life,
God in my lips,
God in my hands,
God in my heart.

Carmina Gadelica

Shepherd Me

Guide of lost sheep,

Herd me to your fold:

Within, safe warmth;

Without, dire cold.

Hook me,

Lift me,

Shepherd me home;

Enclose me,

Hold me,

Lest I roam.

Loving Father

Each thing I have received, from you it came,
Each thing for which I hope, from your love it will come,
Each thing I enjoy, it is of your bounty,
Each thing I ask, comes of your disposing.

Holy God, loving Father, of the word everlasting,
Grant me to have of you this living prayer:
Lighten my understanding, kindle my will, begin my doing,
Incite my love, strengthen my weakness, enfold my desire.

Cleanse my heart, make holy my soul, confirm my faith,
Keep safe my mind and compass my body about;
As I utter my prayer from my mouth,
In my own heart may I feel your presence.

Carmina Gadelica

Friends and Family

Peace to You

The peace of God to you,
The peace of Christ to you,
The peace of Spirit to you,
During all your life,
All the days of your life.

Based on Carmina Gadelica

A Blessing on Children

God's blessing be yours,
And well may it befall you;
Christ's blessing be yours,
And well be you entreated;
Spirit's blessing be yours,
And well spend you your lives,
Each day that you rise up,
Each night that you lie down.

Carmina Gadelica

Blessing on Friend or Family

I pray for you a joyous life,
Honour, estate and good repute,
No sigh from your breast,
No tear from your eye.

No hindrance on your path,
No shadow on your face,
Until you lie down in that mansion,
In the arms of Christ benign.

Carmina Gadelica

God's Aid

Healing Hand

I say the prayer from my mouth,
I say the prayer from my heart,
I say the prayer to you yourself,
O Healing Hand, O Son of the God of our salvation;

To give praise to you, O Jesus,
Lord of sea and of land,
Lord of sun and of moon,
Lord of the beautiful stars.

Put your salve to my sight,
Put your balm to my wounds,
Put your linen robe to my skin,
O Healing Hand, O Son of the God of our salvation.

Carmina Gadelica

God's Flame

Flame of the flames,
Ignite in me,
Light up my dark,
Eternally,
Consuming lies
With verity.

God's Power

God's truth between me and all lies;
God's justice between me and all injustice;
God's strength between me and all defeat;
God's purpose between me and all wavering;
God's tenderness between me and all wounds;
God's love between me and all hate.

O My Encircler

O my encircler,
Shelter me tight;
Deep is the darkness,
Deeper the night.

O my encircler,
Still round me be;
I hear the storm now,
I feel the sea.

O my encircler,
How strong your hold;
Light in the darkness,
Warmth in the cold.

The Lord My Refuge

The Lord is a shelter for the oppressed,
  a refuge in times of trouble.
Those who know your name trust in you,
  for you, O Lord, have never abandoned
  anyone who searches for you.

Psalm 9:9–10

Supplication

O Being of life!
O Being of peace!
O Being of time!
O Being of eternity!
O Being of eternity!

Shepherd me this day,
Relieve my distress,
Enfold me this night,
Pour upon me your grace,
Pour upon me your grace!

Carmina Gadelica

May God Shield Me

May God shield me,
May God fill me,
May God keep me,
May God watch me.

May God bring me
To the land of peace,
To the country of the King,
To the peace of eternity.

Praise to the Father,
Praise to the Son,
Praise to the Spirit,
The Three in One.

Carmina Gadelica

God Be My Light

God of sun,
  Be my God;
God of moon,
  Be my God;
God of stars,
  Be my God.

When day is hazy,
When night is black,
When loveliness is lost,

Be my sun,
Be my moon,
Be my stars,
O God of light and wonder.

Be My Island

O God of gods:

On sea
Be my island,

On land
Be my fortress,

In desert
Be my deep, cool well,

In heat
Be my shade,

In cold
Be my shelter,

In darkness
Be my sure, bright light.

God Aiding You

God aiding you
In lane,
In street,
Through rain,
Through sleet,
Through blue-sky day,
In car,
In coach,
On motorway,
On train,
On plane,
In park in dark,
With stranger's face
In marketplace,
In sunlight
And in lamp post's
Glare,
God aiding you,
God everywhere.

God Guide Me

God guide me with your wisdom,
God chastise me with your justice,
God help me with your mercy,
God protect me with your strength.

God fill me with your fullness,
God shield me with your shade,
God fill me with your grace,
For the sake of your Anointed Son.

Carmina Gadelica

Alone and Frightened

I am here abroad,
I am here in need,
I am here in pain,
I am here in straits,
I am here alone,
O God, aid me.

Carmina Gadelica

House Blessings

A New Dwelling

Be the cross of Christ on your new dwelling,
Be the cross of Christ on your new hearth,
Be the cross of Christ on your new abode,
Upon your new fire blazing.

Carmina Gadelica

Blessing of the House

May God give blessing
To the house that is here;

May the King of the elements
Be its help,
The King of glory
Be near it.

Carmina Gadelica

A House Blessing

Bless, O God, the house,
Bless, O God, the fire,
Bless, O God, the hearth;
May you yourself be our stay.

Carmina Gadelica

Justice, Peace and Reconciliation

Prayer for Justice

Each day may I love your justice,
Each day may I act with your rightness,
Each day may I speak with your wisdom,
Each day may I be at peace with you and my neighbour.
Each day may I remember your mercies,
Each day may I observe your commands,
Each day may I compose a song
To praise you, O God of seas and lands.

Adapted from Carmina Gadelica

Prayer for Reconciliation

Now to the Father who created each creature,
Now to the Son who paid ransom for His people,
Now to the Holy Spirit, Comforter of might:
Shield and deliver us from every wound;
Be about the beginning and end of our race,
Be giving us to sing in glory,
In peace, in rest, in reconciliation,
Where no tear shall be shed, where death comes no more.
Where no tear shall be shed, where death comes no more.

Carmina Gadelica

Marriage

Marriage Blessing

Be your generosity
Like that of the heavenly Father.

Be your love
Like that of the sacrificial Son.

Be your companionship
Like that of the tender Spirit.

Be your forgiveness
Like that of the Great Three,

Until you walk together
The streets of heaven.

Marriage Pledge

I bind myself to you
As I bind myself to Christ:

With truth,
With integrity,
With loyalty,
With constancy.

I bind myself to you
As Christ binds himself to me:

With compassion,
With understanding,
With forgiveness,
With the honour due created life;

Without judgment,
Without hostility,
Without rancour,
Without selfishness.

Our bond, Christ's bond;
Our life, Christ's life;
Our love, Christ's love.

Praise

Praise to the Three

Praise to the Father above us,
Praise to the Son beside us,
Praise to the Spirit within us,
The Three all around us:

The Three of might,
The Three of mirth,
The Three of night,
The Three of bright morn,
The Three of height,
The Three of depth,
The Three of flood,
The Three of ebb tide,
The Three of frost,
The Three of flame,
The Three of quake,
The Three of calm,
The Three of my always longing soul;
Each piece,
Each part,
The whole;

Above, beside,
Within, around,
To my Great Three
Let praise abound.

Praise to Jesu

There is not a plant in the ground
That is not full of His virtue,
There is no mark in the sand
That is not full of His blessing.
Jesu! Jesu! Jesu!
How fitting it is to praise Him.

There is no life in the sea,
There is no creature in the river,
There is nothing beneath the sky
That does not proclaim His goodness.
Jesu! Jesu! Jesu!
How fitting it is to praise Him.

There is no bird on the wing,
There is no star in the sky,
There is nothing beneath the sun
That does not proclaim His goodness.
Jesu! Jesu! Jesu!
How fitting it is to praise Him.

Carmina Gadelica

Thanksgiving

Thanksgiving for all of Life

God of highest heavens,
floating clouds,
God of blue sky,
hot sun,
God of bright, white stars,
sweet moon,
God of soft earth,
biting wind,
God of blazing fire,
gushing waters,
God of solid brick,
smooth stone,
God of all goodness,
tender mercy,
Thank you for all of life today.

And for this my very own life,
Yes, for this my very own life.

Travel

The Journey Blessing

Bless to me, O God,
The earth beneath my foot,
Bless to me, O God,
The path whereon I go;
Bless to me, O God,
The thing of my desire;
Evermore of evermore,
Bless to me my rest.

Carmina Gadelica

Journey Petition

Be a smooth way before me,
Be a guiding star above me,
Be a keen eye behind me,
This day, this night, for ever.

I am weary and forlorn,
Lead me to the land of the angels;
Let me sit in the presence of Christ
And surround myself with the peace of heaven;

O God of all life,
Be at peace with me, be my support,
Be my star, the captain at my wheel,
That I may lie down in peace and rise to life anew.

Carmina Gadelica

Travel by Car...

A blessing on this car (train/plane/boat…).
The Father who watches all
Be with it.

A blessing on this car (train/plane/boat…).
The Son who travelled the hard road to the cross
Be with it.

A blessing on this car (train/plane/boat…).
The Spirit who dwells with us wherever we go
Be with it.

The Father,
The Son,
The Spirit,
To surround and protect this car (train/plane/boat…).

For Peace When Flying

God of unclouded skies,
May the bright clarity of your peace
Dispel the haze of our mistrust;
So that creatures made in your image
(Who, lifted by grace, soar through your heavens)
May not raise evil to such heights.

Keep us free
Above storm,
Above wind,
Above turbulence of rage.

God of unbounded sky,
Give peace,
Peace as we fly.

Travel Blessing

May God make safe to you each steep,
May God make open to you each pass,
May God make clear to you each road,
And may God take you in the clasp
Of God's own two hands.

Carmina Gadelica

Prayer for Travelling

Life be in my speech,
Sense in what I say,
The bloom of cherries on my lips,
Till I come back again.

Carmina Gadelica

God Upon My Track

God before me, God behind me,
God above me, God below me;
I on the path of God,
God upon my track.

Carmina Gadelica

First Line Index